HIDDEN PICTURES

ALL RIGHTS RESERVED
No part of this publication may be reproduced, distributed, or
transmitted in any form or by any means,
including photocopying, recording, or other electronic or
mechanical methods, without the prior written permission
of the publisher, except in the case of brief quotations
embodied in critical reviews and certain other non-commercial
uses permitted by copyright law.

I FOUND IT!

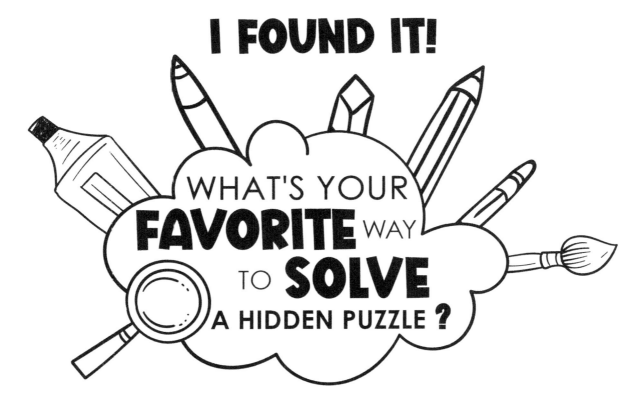

WHAT'S YOUR FAVORITE WAY TO SOLVE A HIDDEN PUZZLE?

There are TONS of different ways, including:

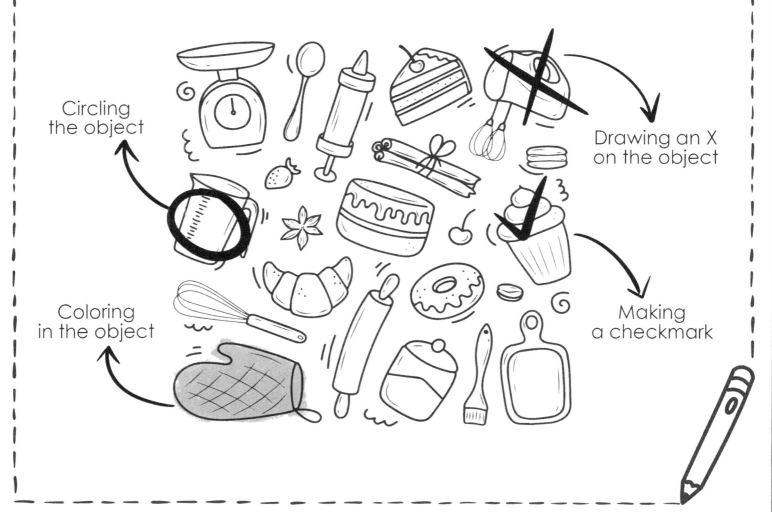

- Circling the object
- Drawing an X on the object
- Coloring in the object
- Making a checkmark

THIS BOOK BELONGS TO

....

....

....

CAN YOU FIND 8 HIDDEN OBJECTS IN THIS SCENE?

3

CAN YOU FIND 8 HIDDEN OBJECTS IN THIS SCENE?

4

CAN YOU FIND 8 HIDDEN OBJECTS IN THIS SCENE?

5

CAN YOU FIND 8 HIDDEN OBJECTS IN THIS SCENE?

6

CAN YOU FIND 8 HIDDEN OBJECTS IN THIS SCENE?

8

CAN YOU FIND 8 HIDDEN OBJECTS IN THIS SCENE?

CAN YOU FIND 8 HIDDEN OBJECTS IN THIS SCENE?

CAN YOU FIND 8 HIDDEN OBJECTS IN THIS SCENE? **13**

CAN YOU FIND 8 HIDDEN OBJECTS IN THIS SCENE? **15**

CAN YOU FIND 8 HIDDEN OBJECTS IN THIS SCENE?

16

CAN YOU FIND 8 HIDDEN OBJECTS IN THIS SCENE? **17**

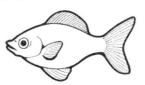   

CAN YOU FIND 8 HIDDEN OBJECTS IN THIS SCENE? **18**

CAN YOU FIND 8 HIDDEN OBJECTS IN THIS SCENE?

19

CAN YOU FIND 8 HIDDEN OBJECTS IN THIS SCENE? **20**

CAN YOU FIND 8 HIDDEN OBJECTS IN THIS SCENE? **22**

CAN YOU FIND 8 HIDDEN OBJECTS IN THIS SCENE? 23

CAN YOU FIND 8 HIDDEN OBJECTS IN THIS SCENE? **25**

CAN YOU FIND 8 HIDDEN OBJECTS IN THIS SCENE? 27

CAN YOU FIND 8 HIDDEN OBJECTS IN THIS SCENE?

28

SOLUTIONS

LET'S CHECK IT OUT! 1

LET'S CHECK IT OUT!

2

LET'S CHECK IT OUT!

3

LET'S CHECK IT OUT!

4

LET'S CHECK IT OUT! 5

LET'S CHECK IT OUT!

6

LET'S CHECK IT OUT!

7

LET'S CHECK IT OUT!

8

LET'S CHECK IT OUT!

LET'S CHECK IT OUT!

10

LET'S CHECK IT OUT!

LET'S CHECK IT OUT!

12

LET'S CHECK IT OUT!

13

LET'S CHECK IT OUT!

LET'S CHECK IT OUT!

15

LET'S CHECK IT OUT!

LET'S CHECK IT OUT!

17

LET'S CHECK IT OUT!

LET'S CHECK IT OUT!

19

LET'S CHECK IT OUT!

20

LET'S CHECK IT OUT!

22

LET'S CHECK IT OUT!

24

LET'S CHECK IT OUT!

25

LET'S CHECK IT OUT!

26

LET'S CHECK IT OUT!

27

LET'S CHECK IT OUT!

28

LET'S CHECK IT OUT!

29

LET'S CHECK IT OUT!

30

WRITE DOWN YOUR FAVORITE ASPECTS OF THIS BOOK:

THANK YOU FOR TRUSTING US BY PURCHASING OUR BOOKS

Your trust in us means a lot, and we truly hope that you will find joy and satisfaction in coloring our unique designs. If our book meets your expectations, we kindly ask you to leave a positive review as it motivates us to create even better books in the future. Once again, thank you for your support and we hope that our coloring book will bring a little bit of creativity and relaxation into your life.